ENVIRONMENTAL CHARITIES AND THEIR WORK

By

JOANNA BRUNDLE

Book Life
King's Lynn
Norfolk PE30 4LS

ISBN: 978-1-78637-311-3

Printed in Malaysia

Written by:
Joanna Brundle

Edited by:
Kirsty Holmes

Designed by:
Gareth Liddington

A catalogue record for this book is available from the British Library.

Photocredits: Abbreviations: l-left, r-right, b-bottom, t-top, c-centre, m-middle. All images are courtesy of Shutterstock.com.

Cover – Tigergallery, 1 – Rakopton TanyakamLPN, 2 – ronnybas, 3 – Alohaflaminggo, 4 – Monkey Business Images, 5 – ProDesign studio, 6 – Tatiana Grozetskaya, 7 – Vlad61, 8 – SOMRERK WITTHAYANANT, 9 – Korelidou Mila, 10 – Rawpixel.com, 11 – Mr Pics, 12 – Kuttelvaserova Stuchelova, 13 – Lenscap Photography, 14 – Fila, 15 – Olena Zaskochenko, 16 – FloridaStock, 17 – vitstudio, 18 – Maciej Olszewski, 19 – Manfred Ruckszio, 20 – varuna, 21 – Patrick Foto, 22 – Pavel L Photo and Video, 23 – Dalibor Danilovic, 24 – A.Srisawang.

Images are courtesy of Shutterstock.com. With thanks to Getty Images, Thinkstock Photo and iStockphoto.

CONTENTS

Words that look like **this** can be found in the glossary on page 24.

Page 4 What Is a Charity?

Page 6 What Does the Environment Need?

Page 8 How Do Environmental Charities Help?

Page 10 How Do Environmental Charities Raise Money?

Page 12 How Is the Money Spent?

Page 14 The Woodland Trust

Page 16 Greenpeace

Page 18 Friends of the Earth

Page 20 How You Can Help

Page 24 Glossary and Index

WHAT IS A CHARITY?

A charity is an **organisation** that supports people, animals or **causes** that need help. Charities need to raise money in order to do this work.

People who work for a charity without being paid are called volunteers.

THESE PEOPLE ARE COLLECTING MONEY FOR A CHARITY.

Collecting money for charities is known as fundraising.

SOME ENVIRONMENTAL CHARITIES WORK TO PROTECT NATURAL AREAS LIKE RAINFORESTS.

There are thousands of charities around the world. Each charity helps a different group in need. Charities do not make a **profit**.

WHAT DOES THE ENVIRONMENT NEED?

Environmental problems include pollution and **global warming**.

POLLUTION IS THE WORD USED FOR HARMFUL THINGS IN THE ENVIRONMENT.

The environment is made up of all natural living and non-living things. It needs protection so that all these things can exist together.

If the environment is not protected, plant, animal and human life can be damaged. Natural **ecosystems** can break down. Places of natural beauty disappear.

WARMER SEAS, CAUSED BY GLOBAL WARMING, CAN DESTROY CORAL REEFS.

A COLOURFUL CORAL REEF

HOW DO ENVIRONMENTAL CHARITIES HELP?

Environmental charities teach people how to protect our planet and to look after natural places like forests and rivers. Some carry out important **research**.

THESE VOLUNTEERS ARE RE-PLANTING A FOREST.

Some organise protests to try to stop things that damage the environment. Some help to deal with environmental disasters, like spills of oil from tankers.

HOW DO ENVIRONMENTAL CHARITIES RAISE MONEY?

Charities use social media to tell people about their work.

CHARITY WEBSITES RAISE MONEY FROM DONATIONS AND ONLINE SHOPS.

Charities raise money by asking for **donations** on television and in magazines. Some pay street collectors who ask people to promise a small, regular donation.

Some people leave money to charities when they die. Others donate through their workplace by giving a small amount of their wages each month.

MARATHON RUNNERS OFTEN RAISE MONEY BY BEING **SPONSORED** TO RUN.

HOW IS THE MONEY SPENT?

Some environmental charities run **conservation** projects, like protecting nature reserves. Charities use advertising to help people think about environmental problems and how they can help.

Charities spend some money on advertisements, to raise more money.

ENVIRONMENTAL CHARITIES WORK TO SAVE ANCIENT FORESTS AND PEAT BOGS.

PEAT BOG

Some charities fund projects that help people live in environmentally friendly ways. The Rainforest Alliance helps people grow crops like bananas without damaging the rainforest.

THE WOODLAND TRUST

THE WOODLAND TRUST PROTECTS WOODLANDS AND THEIR WILDLIFE.

The charity organises lots of children's activities, like bug hunts.

The Woodland Trust is a UK conservation charity that protects ancient forests and plants new woodlands. It also sets up wildlife areas around woodlands.

Trees are very important to the environment. They provide homes and food for wildlife and clean our air by **absorbing** a harmful gas called **carbon dioxide**.

LEAVES FROM A DISEASED CHESTNUT TREE

MANY TREES DIE FROM DISEASES CAUSED BY BUGS AND FUNGI.

The Woodland Trust has planted 36 million new trees since 1972.

GREENPEACE

Greenpeace is an international charity. It tries to protect our planet, including oceans and ancient forests, from environmental damage. Greenpeace also fights against global warming.

GLOBAL WARMING IS MELTING THE ICY HOMES OF POLAR BEARS.

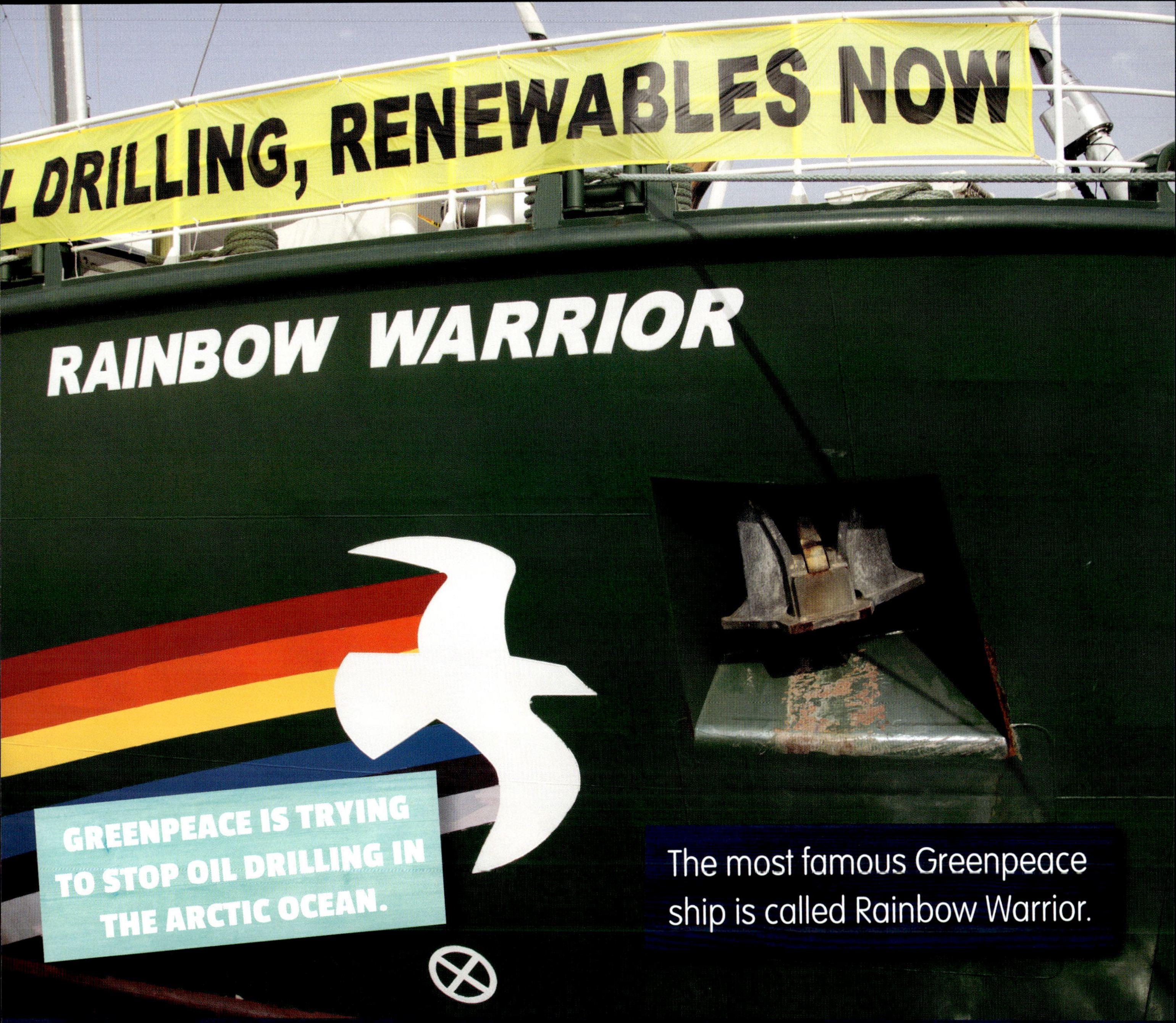

GREENPEACE IS TRYING TO STOP OIL DRILLING IN THE ARCTIC OCEAN.

The most famous Greenpeace ship is called Rainbow Warrior.

Greenpeace funds ships that sail to places where damage to the environment is happening. Volunteers record and film the damage and try to stop it.

FRIENDS OF THE EARTH

THE BUZZ ABOUT BEES

Bees pollinate wild and garden flowers.

SPRAYS USED BY FARMERS TO KILL HARMFUL PESTS ALSO KILL BEES.

Bees are very important to our food supply. As they fly around, bees move pollen between flowering plants. This is called pollination and it helps plants to grow and produce food.

Friends of the Earth is a charity that is helping bees. It plants wildflower areas and has helped to change laws about harmful sprays.

WILDFLOWER MEADOWS ATTRACT BEES AND PROVIDE FOOD FOR THEM.

The charity has planted 200 wildflower Bee Worlds across the UK.

HOW YOU CAN HELP

Find out as much as you can about world environmental problems. Tell people around you and ask them to donate to an environmental charity.

MAKE A COLOURFUL POSTER TO HELP YOU TELL YOUR STORY.

Look on charity websites for news about their work.

Always take your rubbish home with you after a picnic.

CONSERVATION CHARITIES NEED VOLUNTEERS TO COUNT GARDEN BUTTERFLIES AND INSECTS.

You can help with your family by volunteering for a conservation project in your area. Be an environmentally friendly family by turning off taps and lights.

GET ACTIVE!

WEAR GLOVES AND STAY SAFE!

Rubbish damages beaches, clogs up rivers and harms wildlife.

ASK FOR SPONSORSHIP FOR EACH BAG OF LITTER YOU COLLECT.

Why not hold a sponsored litter collection with your family and friends? You will be helping the environment and raising money at the same time.

Decorate a charity money box at home. Ask people to donate spare coins. Charge fines for actions that damage the environment, like forgetting to recycle rubbish.

A LANDFILL SITE FOR RUBBISH

RECYCLING RUBBISH HELPS TO STOP ENVIRONMENTAL DAMAGE LIKE THIS.

Paper, cans and bottles can all be recycled.

GLOSSARY

absorbing	taking in or soaking up
carbon dioxide	a natural, colourless gas found in the air
causes	issues that people are concerned about and want to support
conservation	protection of the natural environment
donations	things that are given to a charity, especially money
ecosystems	a community of living things and their environment
global warming	the slow rise of the Earth's temperature, caused by burning fuels like coal and oil
organisation	a group of people, such as a club or charity, with a particular purpose
profit	money made by a business after all its costs have been paid
research	tests and experiments to find out information
sponsored	promised money by a supporter to complete an activity such as a marathon

INDEX

conservation 12, 14, 21
donations 10-11, 20, 23
Friends of the Earth 18-19
fundraising 5, 10-11, 22
global warming 6-7, 16
Greenpeace 16-17
pollution 6, 15
Rainforest Alliance 13
volunteers 4, 8, 17, 21
Woodland Trust 14-15